Little Empires

Little Empires

Robert Colman

QUATTRO BOOKS

The publication of *Little Empires* has been generously supported by the Canada Council for the Arts and the Ontario Arts Council.

Some of these poems were previously published in the following journals: *CV2, Exile Quarterly, Existere, Nashwaak Review, Queen's Quarterly, The Malahat Review, The Toronto Quarterly*, and *The Windsor Review.*

Author's photograph: Kristi Cross
Cover painting: detail from *Constellation Fire* by Viktor Mitic
Cover design: Diane Mascherin
Editor: Allan Briesmaster

Library and Archives Canada Cataloguing in Publication

Colman, Robert
Little empires / Robert Colman.

Poems.

Issued also in an electronic format.

ISBN 978-1-927443-02-6

I. Title.

PS8605.O473L58 2012 C811'.6 C2012-903910-1

Published by Quattro Books Inc.
382 College Street
Toronto, Ontario, M5T 1S8
www.quattrobooks.ca

Printed in Canada

For Kristi

Contents

III.

IV.

Little Empire

after Jack Chambers' Lunch (unfinished) 1969

When you painted the linear cleanliness
of your family presiding over Sunday lunch,
was it really, as some critics say,
divine inspiration, with Jesus about to appear
at the empty chair on your right?

The joyous kingdom of the steady,
the sated, you suggest, is in this
focus – scrubbed walls,
neatly ordered snow,
and the one lily thriving
in an aura's smudge of light.

Yet, you left it unfinished, and we can't
not ask why. The riddle of
Persian rug you insisted be included?
Illness? Avoiding its purchase?
Nine years, no conclusion.

But what would it be, completed?
The glory of empire, holy or lay,
is the marshaled troops,
the choir-sung hymns,
the peak not yet reached
but in view. Here,

the room is still breathing into colour,
the reflections in the eyes of your two boys
unfocused but sharpening,
wanting so much to see.

I.

Hunger

Ghost dogs slaver among the thickets
of houses tracking our discontent.
You think you know hunger
until you hear those red jaws,
muscle drowning reason.

Your version of the word
is something else altogether.
You wish for satiation,
a kyanite explosion of blue
ocean returned to you
again and again, warm and weighty.

But those waves keep washing you back
to the sound of dogs, their blades
of lungs you've no answer for,
no locks for the doors you open,
senseless of what to let in,
what to keep out.

Cover Version (Hong Kong)

Bridge Over Troubled Water falters
in the lounge of the Marriott, the band
expanding it a little too far,
not understanding it's reserve
that Garfunkel works,
precarious balance.

My lychee martini is too boozy,
so I'm chewing cashews, staring
into icicles of neon and glass,
a ricochet through the harbour.

I've wandered the city all day, watching
nannies picnic in the park,
street preachers fencing pamphlets,
everyone on cell phones, conjuring

home. What we breathe
is sea, refuse, dried scallops, exhaust,
and the sharper tang of air con
on overdrive. Everything new
already mired, misused –
a knock-off, bored perfection.

I'd dump the drink but can't think
what to do besides sit and chew, and sip,
and hear song after song blunted
against the fug of night.

The Set-Up

Impossible wooden brides draped
in cotton-mouthed pinks and sea-lit greens
chide me from your shop window.
Ignorant of names, I chafe
against their wordless
jeweled throats.

This is you. I form *you*
from ghosts.

My back spasms and I wince myself
out of the wishing, wonder
if meeting you will be a sharp departure.
Does our baggage dash any chances,
and have I always misconstrued sacrifice?
What will I make of it this time?

Pathetic patter, this desire
for *full*, or *other*.

The past stacks its fires high, of course,
as if to preserve in its encampment something almost had.
But I'm told I'll like you, and keep staring
into the store's heart, summoning
a belief in stone and hard rains.

Pretty punks straddle the corner talking smack,
a spit of me wanting a smart remark,
spoiling for a fist. But nothing takes.

I talk myself out of invention,
spare you the collar of expectation.

Meeting

This is not a fever heat, waiting
for frenzy to subside into sense.
Don't even call it curiosity.

Just a customer,
the alacrity of his handshake,
coffee and cinnamon introduction.

This is nothing more –
polishing the glass of
her display,

correcting the fall
of silver and stone.
This is her hand

busying out that gesture,
his palm's confident press.
She is practicing

the only touch she believes in right now.
The quietude of elegance
carefully cut and strung.

For Sale (After the Failure of the Expansionist Dream)

The horizon buckles closed.
The world, bending beyond sight –
today a grocery store, card shop,
leather-crowded cobbler's kiosk.

The rest is pebbledash, wood lathe and plaster,
a scuffed, shucked 10-pin alley. My daily walk,
past a glass house of fire engines,
arrow-fit office windows.
I imagine zombies in the barren parking lots,

and what freedom means, and success,
whether the scratch of a pen can compute even one,
if thought alone could ever suffice.
The buildings look the other way,
pretend to be elsewhere, whistling dust.

The Bees

He left the over-air-conditioned office. Suddenly his legs were longer and he didn't feel so fat. He sat in his steam-heated car and thawed. Thawed for ten minutes or more before the heat seemed to register beneath his freckle-burnt skin. *Like frostbite in mid-summer*, he thought, opening the car door. In control as he felt, it was like the order of one thin string running the length of him, one shoelace he wound and unwound daily, fraying further by the hour. Back in the office, the tea didn't help but it sent him walking, which seemed important. People would stop to talk and he could hover, bee-like for a minute or two, humming around the sound of them, the echo of himself in them. It was good, and also bad. Essence is too strong a word, but the bee feeling hovered in the ballpark of such a sentiment, something he didn't want to own so completely. The car was a good place to be. He could gaze out over the plaza, meekly imagine himself above it, holding a small audience captive just by displaying a bit of dazzle, some of that razzmatazz frozen within him some time ago – the part of him that could ignore the hollow thrum of his ghost, its string-thin voice repeating *me, me, me*.

Concerto

Tone rows boat out of a dissipating rain,
an arrhythmic introduction to the city.

People are sleeping behind the wheel,
phones on hands-free. Hear the burble

threading along the iron posts of patios.
Heat rises from the cement, gets trapped

at the ankles. We wade into its bass notes.
I am starved for the line, clammy-palmed.

Your hair is the cello, a hushed patience.
I'm a bow's length from further interpretation.

You are beautiful by basic definition,
asking me to parallel park the car.

Who are you? the poet asks his student,
looking for the chosen essence.

I had this idea you would tell me
a piece of this, a bar of my sound,

a quantity or progression I might have
drawn from me. There are uncertain violins

now, opening the self-lie. You remain
safe on the other edge of the sidewalk.

If I don't think of you

I walk the mall parking lot at noon,
stalling for time, tracking fissured veins
of tar and the newer sidewalks' white
clam-shell shine – shards of light,
sharpened heat against yielding eyelids.

Legs, set too solid, strain in their flex,
tethered to my shoes' shush and slap –
a machine set for obsolescence
headed towards the bookstore
to scan the magazines, glean
my name among the glossies.

The sky is pool blue lie, nothing
left of my skin when I heft the door open –
sandpaper and doubt, blunt bones of face,
jaw. Joints seized in torn tired clothes,
cutting away the traces, leaving
no idea of love unforgotten.

Cacophony

Everything's too loud. The subway
a concussion at the edge of the road. Toes
rubbing against cotton sheets dragging
a hiss of spine, neck locked in
shiver. Don't even speak of rain
or slippers on carpet. I cringe.
It's the wanting that worries me,
the need behind every noise –
a whole city of small feet.
I open, I shut. I open again.
Such bad musicians,
people, notes piercing
holes in the air.

Recession Blues 1: Shot

Too warm for the snow shearing
from branches in the square, a Japanese cherry's
thick ruff of white on the wind.

I see the camera now, teen actors
preening playful in coutured wool,
colourful and free. Closer,
the fake flakes smell
of fluoride, a detergent wash.
A Golden Lab paws the scent.

A woman, all business, eyes set dead
ahead, marches through the drifts,
determined not to permit surprise.

Early for a meeting, I'm unsure
of my appearance as capable partner,
gun-savvy industry steward. *Pause.*
Breathe. There's money here. I've time

to calm myself, browse some remainders,
busy the fingers. *Be brief,*
unclutter, explain
the value. This I know.

The kids are running repetitions
down a small hill, in slow motion,
in a way we almost never did –
matching, unmarked. The dog
wavers mid-lick.

I tug and straighten my loud blue tie
at the edge. *Smile.*
Fake what you must.

The Artist's Son Speaks of Love

My mother cured me of any wish to be bohemian.
The word smacks of irresponsibility,
carelessness, a vague notion of
an even vaguer "right" to freedom.
What is the world if not structures of decisions
which, naturally, lead to other decisions
that muster, in time, this sense of self-worth.

I choose every possession with equivalent care –
this starched and pearl-buttoned white shirt,
this set of sterling silver cufflinks,
my quietly elegant Italian shoes.

You see this fountain pen,
the remarkable balance of it
when held in the heart of your hand?
That also gives it its flow and passion,
its fine anger. If I cut my mother's photo
to remove my stepfather's hideous mug
I will do that with precision too.

I appreciate my self-imposed limitations,
they are a comfort, and a satisfaction. But
I honour and respect nothing more than
sacrifice, that much-maligned necessity.

Cha, I Love You and Always Will

An inscription, writ by Linda, Christmas '96,
foot of the first page of Paul Durcan's
Christmas Day, his celebration
of woman-hunger and bromance.

Each time you open it, this lost link,
random failure incised
in the copy you found
among other anxious voices
papering a used bookshop.

What made him sell her words?

Unless Linda, a chancer, wrote her love
a game of hide-and-seek,
inscribing random tracts
of that same block letter sentiment.

Would he find her words to him
in a slim volume of pulp lust,
Mao's persistent *Little Red Book*,
the instructive *Erotic Wiles of Roses*,
Durcan's pining *Christmas*
or the doorstopper novel so full of Cha
she was run through with Cha-hunger?

Linda might still await
the right man (or woman – why not?)
caught short by bold statement –
half-inch square capitals so firm and orderly
under Durcan's fragile skin, a woman
who knows you are weak but worth
your puddle, your red scarves of woe.

She is waiting in the snow now,
outside the cemetery, to hold your hand,
knit you a hat, make love to you
on your back, in the blizzard,
in the mess you call your day.

It is okay for her to date you,
Christmas, circa 2010 – she has
her convictions, she can show you,
by heaven, she will, Cha be damned!

And how you want her to
even now, how you do.

Spring Melt

I wet vac the basement every few hours,
watch water saunter back to the dry spaces
even as I pack it in after a few tubs-worth,
trying not to think of Sisyphus with his rock
footing about the foundations.

Had a drink with a friend today
but the conversations get shorter
as his search for work goes sour.
He doesn't want to hear whingeing
from a warmed-over desk jockey.

We end up in a wash of beer,
our eyes on the warm spring sun,
bringing the buzz on without comfort,
propped up at the patio bar, slowly sozzled
in our differences, holding on –

our attempt to move that old rock
without pushing. Like I am, seated upstairs
simmering on about all the water rushing in,
waiting for a less weary me to arrive,
that productive, better man.

Parrot

Hello Sophie, the parrot
cajoles an umpteenth time,
a favourite entry in
her catalogue of greetings
– demi-crescendos of saucy
whistle, pieces of other birds –
lisp of a sparrow, a cardinal's
persistent prayers, and

You're a brat!

borrowed from a 12-year-old girl.

The occasional ugly squawk
I liken to a rook or crow,
but maybe it's the voice
behind the voices, I can't say.
Shame on me, claiming beauty's
rule – one mimic belittling another.

The pattern of her patter shifts
with each flourished to-do,
a cool marble eye cocked my way
as if to say, *Maybe this time*
I'll get through.

II.

The Architect

The house I designed encompassed
all I'd hoped we'd be –
its sitting room a cave of light,
stained glass windows
narrating the passing day
and the creak of hardwood
ushering us to bed.

But the city expropriated the land
to build a new subway entrance,
so I shelved the plans.
Still, I thought, it's at least
something, the sweat of so many
bodies pushing against the rush –
the effort we require to stay true.

Then the civic leaders re-imagined it
into a light rail route terminus
and I thought, why not? Progress
and a cul-de-sac of sure arrival,
the hard lines we all need sometimes.

Nothing's happened, though.
After the election, they rethought the car,
revisited the value of locomotion *in toto*.
I visit the spot every day – weeds yea-high,
beer-bottle buttressed, but thriving. Somehow
I could abide other visions. Not this.

Amid the Bud labels, one lavender flower
draws the eye. Precisely what I fight against,
cloying impermanence, there to be picked,
not true resilience in the least. Just
the city interrupted by a season,
a tease.

So now I must wait,
and you remind me
this is also love,
the hardest kind.

Easter Sunday

is lunch with your ex-husband,
his birthday shot with holy sun
and me left obsessing over
a pagan's uncertain rhymes.

The poem puffs itself up, wheezes
a gasp in the bare March branches.
And when you feed me reassurance
at dinner, my belly does the same.
Making love to you should prove
some point. Pray

I don't sag or shrivel away.
Let's go out walking, across
the sheets of sun-burnt snow,
delicate sheen of warmth,
easily cracked halo.

On Ownership

The house is slick with an ice that has
locked its jaws on the windows and doors.
A key snaps in the cold.

The cat curls itself
inwards like a mollusk,
delicate shell of sleep.

We think we have practiced
winter often enough
but bleed light carelessly, claiming
the dark, grubstake prospectors.

I scour the Web
to decode what ails you,
lull you to sleep
massaging your neck.

Trucks waken you from a light doze.
I am reading beside you, a history
of the Congo and the atrocities of empire,

imagining a man sliding
across a slim sidewalk of ice
outside what he thinks
is his.

Burnout

Sorry I'm late, boss,
but my cat has learned a new trick,
placing his paws on the arm of a chair
Sphinx-like, staring
out into the garden.
No wauling over squirrels.
He leans into the stillness,
that soft-eyed, focused concentration
I never did master in kung-fu.

The feature would have been done
but I was distracted
by a newspaper in the rain,
not just wet but half-macerated,
chewed by the deluge. It put me
in that *why bother* kind of mood.

The online broadcast?
The voice is clear but
would you believe I wore yellow,
so close in the spectrum to
green screen, the cropped me
kept fading out like a recurring echo,
never quite coming into focus.

Clearing the Yard

Saturday is for striking clear
the first stubborn spines of spring,
fleet-figured weeds filling space
that waits for blossom and scent – sour
choke of Rhubarb, stiff cuff of Hosta.

Because of you, this year
is for fixing, laying
stonework, cement,
assessing the sunniest patches of yard,
allowing more.

As you sift the day's stories
I pluck maple sprouts
from the red rock path
and listen to you talk about
friends, their orbiting needs.

Gradually you join me,
twisting thin sprigs of green
between your fingers. Drifting
into an unconscious *doing for*.
I think, *Try hard*

not to imagine more, shake
the dusty leaves, never
assume arrival.
But you are here now.
That is a start.

From the Antique Mall

Among all the bric-a-brac
we choose two clocks to wind
in the subtle lisp of shoppers
shuffling the aisles.
You gift them to me
and I find you

a cocktail shaker in Bakelite green,
a Barbie brush that draws
childhood doors. You tug
these strands of the past
but stay perched in our moment.

I watch you eye the lockets,
linger over what could be
a match for your own heart
clasp. Coming home with our
two clocks, their fat, sturdy hands,
slick curve of metal, thick glass.

I wind them only once,
satisfied more with their silence,
firm bellies of time
holding their breath.

Love

You throw the word, a javelin.
It spins, soars. Cuts the hum
of its purpose.

Am I the ground to grip
or just oxygen that can't but
quiver against its singing?

The Onion Harvest

The photo you took conjures
mineral sweetness stored snugly
in wooden crates
stacked at the side of the path.
Row on row, the smell solid, pungent –
earth, geometrically magnified.

I asked to take an early autumn drive
to unmake our weekend habits,
shake out the blanket of us.
Silent with you out here,
watching as you weigh the landscape,
the nails in the crates, the weathered planks,
empty furrows reasoning out the marsh.

I've run out of questions for you
or can't jaw the language to ask.

I believe we come home happier, having
travelled that flat expanse of industry,
snapping a few stills, talking little,
our hands consciously our own.

Paper skins and rough worn flesh.
A sharp taste we ask
to linger.

A Knight Errant

Something consumed you
tonight, a whiff of spite
in your kisses. Silence
slid onto a tongue
tied to a thought, then
slipped back inside.

Was it some press of gale
against your faith?
A shingle set askew?
Let me take it,
shim it back its space,

hell, hammer it down
with a mace. Gladly
I'll get medieval for you.

Just tell me why.

Recession Blues 2: Committee

The dingy carpet,
plasticized teak veneer –
not a stillness, not eloquent
silence. Like a dog whistle,
ones and zeroes hum above earshot
through the office, folding their heat
in curt commands.

An invitation to the boardroom
where we metamorphose,
become amateur throat singers,
pre-historic matinee idols.
Not apathetic –
resigned to the moment,
the sour accountant's redline
predestined in our watery eyes.

But there is language, and then
there is meaning, and rooms where the two
chase each other to ground. I dream
a sleek tuxedo of sound – horsehair,
wind and ivory – while listening
as everyone warbles flat,
the first violinist a tone-deaf squeal.

Yet I heard the flutes last night at five,
a crescendo of sunset, reverberating
their coda, the last notes of my lost solo.

Still Life

The bowl we had our berries in
still rests on the bedside table,
spoons stacked atop one another,
the seedy flesh of strawberry
a sticky film in its shallow base.

You called this romantic –
the first I'd heard you use the word,
sidling two sweet halves to my lips.

I am listening to Mary Oliver read
how the ear bone is what lasts longest
in each of us, busy thinking of
what we so easily lose within.

You ask me whether I crave
unique experience – material for my work.
And yes, sometimes it's true
I forget to see.

Playing the Edges

I've been staring at your friend Jim's photo
for hours – of you, shooting
a wheat field on a grey day,
hair and jacket, auburn and blue
bleeding into a purple aura
warming the dampness.
To the left, he has found
a finger of colour
among the yellow stalks,
an echo of your body.

No surprise, I'm jealous.
Only a poet, playing the edges,
an "I" bulling its way between the lines
when someone else walks in saying
here you are, a flame
spreading across the landscape.

I get close to something this full
sometimes, capture you
as you divide the view
into its perfect thirds. Not quite art,
you say of the way you work the lens,
then push fieldriot, shutter
silvered bark, etching blue,
feeding on the riven edges.

But this is not quite you. Just a measure
of cedar given to switch grass
given to bees and a few bloated
blossoms mottling the undergrowth.
Nowhere for the settled pen,
though I feel near that spark of self.

So I fumble for the matches
in my pocket, a thin stick of breath
waiting to burn for you.

The Keyboardist

Passion, churned to a few beats
of sharpened being – hip-jerk,
come-shot. Lust
tethered on the whip-crack
slap of a hand turned paw, turned
single finger, teasing the keys.
Want's subtle satisfaction, toying
every desperate second.

Waiting for You

Sometimes I wake to a ruckus of hooves,
sometimes only the dog's awkward breath,
the whispers of thieves. The house, a stranger,
hauls me from sleep.

I find your fingers splayed, warm, open
inches from my face, your arm sprawled
across the impossible expanse of bed.

The grass bows, hears the beaten earth
hum the flanks that susurrate above it –
a silence, then restless hooves again.
And you keep sleeping, exhausted,
too used to chasing night.

Being New

Somewhere on the streets of Chatham
you encounter my past.
Never sure how it happens – the ghosts
gather about you like damp wind
gusting and clinging, wanting
every wrinkle of our bodies, making us
rough with nothingness. So you ask

What was it like with other women?
Where did they take you?
What did they say?

At times I wish I was a virgin again,
washed of the weight of having done and seen.
How perfect, to be without history.
In a tired moment over the sink
clutching a glass of cranberry, knocking it back,
I want it all gone – no memory,
no repetition of old stories,
no me, slack with use.

But that's like begging childhood.
What I give is the moment –
the mirth I take, watching you
marshal the flea market, a gasp
at the sight of TJ Maxx,
how I admire you at your craft – coaxing
the grain from wooden footbridges,
punching up the blue sky
in the rough fist of your lens.

Being new gets more difficult
but is hardly an arduous task.
Harder to explain than to live.
The nuance of being what you insist
of me, and I you. Being flesh, being present.
Believing it true.

The Grounding Stone

I.

Nylon strings of rain, delicate
clefs of vines, taut hollow
awning above our plates.
Raclette spills across my knuckles
as I try to answer the question
your silence asks. *Who* is *he?*
Montréal is lonely,
the language of others
traced in my mind.

I'm all caution with us alone,
this city known but unknown
for us. It could go either way –
if the rain lets up, if it doesn't.
If the past comes pattering
through a mistaken confidence.
We sink a bottle of red and
what do I expect? Ultimatum,
adieu? You wouldn't be here
if you didn't want to.

Trust. I'd love to
ring it up, tell it we're patioed,
prepared for our intro.
I thought it was an absolute,
present or absent.
Now I check my shoes
each morning, the mailbox,
your voice messages
for a sign.

What does *earn* really mean?

II.

I pause in the toilets, stare
at four framed photos –
cows given glamour
in the soft lens. Bucolic glow.
Even they would know better.
So much back and forth
the past few months, I wonder.

And then you're suddenly no distance,
coffee and smoky quartz gaze
laid before me, cracked faith
washed away in the rain.
No questions, no sarcasm,
no language to obfuscate.
Your smile has opened
that ache of a fraction.

Was it the dash from hotel to cab,
our own little Red Sea moment?
Slipping across the seat together?
Or was it just the wine?

III.

You dip a spoon in my bowl of nougat
and I'm beggared for a word –
can't call it joy, this quiet,
the cowardly lion arrived.

I look at my mug in the mirror
every morning, wondering
how anyone gets from A to B
without compass, shaman,
a mother's directions.

Yet B is in sight, somehow,
suddenly allowed now,
your hand in mine, and me
looking for the grounding stone,
that mystical figment,
which *must* be close by.

I've yet to catch up, I realize.
Surely I'd see it, otherwise.

III.

The Emperor, Now a Citizen, Digs His First Hole

Please, don't see this as grand
political statement.

When you are born of heaven
you are not allowed to touch the earth

and you begin to believe in that separation
– so many screens, so many servants

that the barriers themselves become invisible,
organic necessities, like breath

and the reedy steel of my young, sure voice.
Even in their solitary chambers

mind and body assume their preset roles.
The shovel appeared an improbable artifact,

my hands the same. Don't deny
you have been taken unawares like this,

muscles awoken and at once accountable,
in an instant introduced to their own militancy.

But if there is civil strife today
it is between me and the rose garden.

One might use words like "worth" or "purpose."
I prefer "surprise" – an ungoverned emotion.

Sex and the City

Clouds, snow and streetlights
devise a faux Aurora Borealis
across town, warm green-yellow haze
masking the darkness, the sky
made a washed backdrop for
Victorian brownstones, ethereal
as the automotive age will allow.

I've left you at home on the couch,
watching a dramedy
dedicated to the mating habits of
urban women who, like every poet,
would like to think they've hit
upon a new path to the altar,
only to find a lineup for tickets
and scalpers raising the stakes.

I am admiring the neighbourhood Christmas
decorations in a late December thaw –
penguins sleighing the backs of bears,
a snow elephant supine in a laneway,
electric blue bulbs brazing
a spruce silhouette,
and clutter-free colonial windows –
on the sill of each, one joy-
fearing white candle.

The silence is almost absolute,
save the snow-press clumping of my boots,
and above the heads of lovers and families,
ice-melt from a roof corner tap-tap-tapping,
enlarged with every beat until it is a father
with a hammer and a handful of nails,
bothering a persistent leak beneath
the eaves, strung so perfectly in white and red.

Cleanliness: A Guide

Love the hum of the vacuum
across the back hatch of the van.
Scrape the tough carpet with the hose,
raising it once again to new.
Just space – no camping gear, crumbs,
dust-moted decorative pillows.

Spend your hours practicing
clean living – baize-like lawn,
indexed bookshelves, spotless inbox.
Let the doer disappear
behind each silence.

Let nothing disturb your eating.
Chew slowly, as if a marble or stone
were there in the mix to test you.
Think of others' misfortunes, if it paces you.
These you can discard with dessert.

Now listen to the night,
cutlery clanking in the sink,
stacked dishes clicking into place.
Don't talk. Keep to the task at hand,
only the air conditioner loudly spinning
its blades, insolent, efficient.

Recession Blues 3: Tech Offensive

File the filler, film the feature,
Tweet it, Face it, Digg it deep,
make it sticky, make it sweet,
a number north of what we beat
last month, last week. Then, repeat.

At 9 a.m. I talk a colleague down to calm,
mock the shop talk that only ends in noise.
We devise a prison break, of sorts,
before the day takes hold – decide
that we are human, meaning
we should entrust our souls to dogs,
beyond the bubble-wrap pop of
instant messages, whisper them

our plans for escape – on bicycles
burning rubber into autumn breezes,
pedals hugging the weight of our heels.
I can't speak for my colleague
but I've got my eye on a shiny
blue two-wheeler, old-fashioned,
with a basket for my shopping
and a strident silver bell
to carry me through traffic.

Awaiting The Axe

Sometimes the sound of the river
isn't clue enough. Fiddling
your fingers in its brackish shallows
doesn't give away its scent
or tempt you closer to understanding
the current. You've paddled
as far as strength will allow
and still true eludes you.

So you stop, or almost so,
build a dock, a bridge of sticks,
then mix a gin and tonic,
cross your ankles and doze.
No more forward, no back,

just waiting for the ring of a telephone,
a voice trained in neutral.

Ice cracks loudly in your glass.
You crave the sound of breaking.

Packing for a conference

requires more than remembering
the toothpaste for thinning enamel
or a security-safe tube of hair product.
I must predict or recall the psyche
balled up regularly in that suitcase –
business card wedged in the ID slot,
heart and mind shoved between the shirts.

So I set out my fellow travellers –
Kleinzahler or Oliver?
Tricky, choosing either
peacekeeper or co-conspirator.
Will I need escape or companionship?
Difficult to know who I'll be.

If I ask the man at the corner of the hotel bar
he'd likely insist on Poe,
a misanthrope's romantic elixir,
while the bartender might want Frost,
his snowed-in tracks, brambled path.

But when I reach the airport lounge,
its blue glass, flat screens, safely wanded air,
I am searching for Ted Kooser who,
just now, walked his dog out of the pre-dawn,
a snowstorm and its aftermath glistening
harmlessly on his broad, wondering smile.

The Hopes of a Nascent Nation

Still a loose confederation,
its rulers debate the flag.
What shall it embody –
Civility? Protection? Brotherhood?
Love is wrapped in there, yes,
but it's too cliché to trumpet.

All the best colours have been taken
or have suffered the abuses of fashion.
They settle for beige,
with accents.

The commander-in-chief is working
on the Wikipedia entry, to solidify
their international standing.
He believes, but in his closet
keeps a bag packed at the ready.

Hush

From the lake we snake a path
among the old clap cottages. Town.
Thick and trim lawns, stricken
with the switch and run of mowers,
doused in novocaine street lamps.

Families mime behind picture windows
their complicated *whys*.
An old woman rug-hooks her days
behind a hedge of white planters.
A fallen bird's nest is filigree now,
the hem of wild frayed to a breath.

We carry coffees to keep warm,
imagining this filament hum
as fulfillment, square and set,
Cary Grant come to finish the story.
You crawl my hand in your cuff,
pinch my wrist, tentative, rousing me
as the trees exhale their chatter.

Starfish

The sandflats silt a trail of shallows
we haul and sloop ourselves through.
The tide pull took us out paddle-less
and we stretch our return in easier waters,
looping a path through the tide grass,
sink our oars deep in the sand 'til I voice
a concern for the cautious crabs beneath.
So we shim-slip the surface, slow and
steady, seldom dragging the keel
against the wet grain.

We see little that is alive –
a parade of periwinkles,
small colony of hermits.
Not even a weave of minnows
wrinkles the stillness.
But then – a starfish
slyly adjusting its grip on a rock,
an almost imperceptible ripple of limbs
shifting into a more careful position.

I only understood them as string-
bagged decoration, suburban accessory.
And now the creature lifts what might be
a knuckle, flexing then folding
around itself again, signalling
a cautious greeting.

I would have liked to touch it.
I wanted to feel it breathe,
how it might grip me.

But you would have stopped me.
And who knows how far
I'd have had to fall
to reach it?

Caught

for Andrew

I saw you in the churchyard
late last night, digging up bones
for your next beneficent work of art.
It put me in mind of Stanley Spencer –
his Nativity scene, the one wise man
paying the baby Jesus some mind.

Don't be embarrassed to be caught.
I like how you handle the weightlessness
of each shin and scapula, severing
connection, reconstituting the self –
what creation is really all about.

To speak of obscenities doesn't make sense
these days. Not as if we choose
our ideas of perfection, slumming
in enthusiasm's old graveyard. Protection,
those claymores you mentioned,
maybe that's what we need.

I've got a bottle of Bordeaux,
some soft cheese and baguettes in tow.
Forget the pressed suit and hair gel,
the morning papers' angst as well.
Don't brand it bonding; I'm just here
reminding you of meaning, how easy

it is to murder. But you know.
I repeat it for myself, as you dig and sift,
and the skeletons clap their hands,
the rhythm they smack out
so damned familiar, I reach for a spade
to tap along, recall the refrain.

I concentrate on the rattling blues
and thank God you hear it, too.
It's akin to safety, feeding the dark
what I brought with me –
those doubts
just a grave away.

Painting the Storeroom

Mat Kearney is turning rap into a dirge.
We sing or hum along until the final tune –
the saddest, you say.

Maybe we'd broken up last time you heard it.
Hard to know. But it echoes with the slap of
paintbrushes squaring the small space.

I slip my brush around loose metal wire,
phone cords, pipes capped cleanly
in a dull yellow beige. The room reeks

continuity – what I don't yet know.
Keeping love, coaxing it, worried
there will be another break.

As you finish off the rolling, I rinse
the brushes, press them to the basin,
flick the bristles in the murky wash.

We aren't satisfied when we're done.
You expected something pristine.
I hadn't thought to bet on anything.

Labradorite – A Meditation

I. Stone

Coiled scale, oil slick, cracked
mantle of storm made solid.
Victorian Thames, cigar smoke,
gaslight in a jar.

II. Definition

Restive, she left the apartment,
November tungsten bulbs
singeing the damp. The point
only to roil herself, exercise, repeat
the movements her sifu taught,
even now, walking in the rain:

how a sharp flicked wrist
is velocity and surprise,
how gravity serves its purpose,
and that memory is also physical.

Twist, feint, wick the rain away,
her fist an imitation of animal
instinct – tiger, snake, eagle – a wing
that is blade and momentum.

From a distance, her hands dance
and fidget. It is hard to see method,
form and safety.

III. Honing the light

You
the Thames,
gaslight, flick and feint,
a wing remembered sideways
as from peripheral flight.
Then a flash, wick-wristed,
the body's learned gravity
become a new velocity.

IV.

Dr. Tsien Responds to His Biographers

Perhaps I should be proud, the silk
weave of my career captured, embossed,
sewn between covers. My life
an ineluctable arc of 20th century –

McCarthy, missile proliferation,
Mao muddied in political dreams,
a corolla of condemnations, the dead
flower of our Great Leap Forward.

Then, finally, a kind of ascension,
qualified by accusations
I had turned tail on friends,
achieving only hollow heights.

Of course I am angry.
Understand, survival is a skill,
unlearning a chosen culture
to embody the civic symbol

until your shoulders loosen
in the shell of this new self,
though your lips taste bitter
knowing. I did not write this story.

That is your arrogance. Believing
in your linear code.
I can't argue that from you, nor
do I ask for pity.

It made sense (family, safety)
to want a simplified landscape,
a mathematical world, basic
equations ordering our lives.

It had a kind of purpose, shouting
the ugly sparrows from their perches,
chasing them from every surface until
they expired of fright, exhausted.

You, too, will seem ridiculous
in others' eyes, calling forth
the fragile bones of ghosts,
searching for some true history.

Herdwick Sheep

for Chris

They are very sweet, he said,
and I pictured meat, glazed in mint,
the Norse consonants softened
to stew. But he continued,

If I were to date a sheep,
it'd be a Herdy.
Such gentle temperaments.

If the bilberries had been bruising summer
he'd have broken one pensively
against his tongue, following
fell to waterfall with his eyes.

See that gill there, meandering
a slow switchback through the fields?

No mention of the Swaledales or Roughs
in his speech, no discussion of the tups,
yet not a touch of the Hesket brew on his breath.

A river the way it's meant, not yet unbent
by farmers mad for one more arable inch,
ignorant of water, gravity's cut winch.

And he said *date,* as if to wait attendance
at the edge of her heaf, ruddying up
his countenance, a gentleman to the teeth.

There's a Herdwick now, grazing
close to the path. She'll slowly age
to gray from that young coat of black.

A fond gaze – at root, this place
in his respectful, quiet
seeing. The skin shorn clean
of its fictions of distances.

Bigfoot Cured My Arthritis

I was no different from the rest,
only beyond weak as he walked the clearing.
Crippled up, cut from fear, I said,
"Alright, I'm all yours to gut or throw,
I'm all tapped out."

And that's when he rested
the weight of his arms on mine,
a warmth wriggling free
of the cold threat of air.

I was awestruck at the root
of his magic, those imposing, slab-like hands,
the matted fur, the smell of him
working through my joints.

Just placing my palm in his
was monumental, another idea –
not really a hand at all.
A form of mythology that heals
by proving itself true.

Respect

The pine cone is so dry,
its tips like sculpted bone,
the mystery of design given way
to the marvel of decay and, perhaps,
some semblance of return.
It is impossible not to be
enamoured of cycles, the body
enlivened by living them, knowing
winter as a hunger that passes.

But what of belief? And respect?
Where do these fit
in the trunk of my car,
beside the jack, the diminutive
spare tire?

I suppose I believe in return
on a grand scale, though I often fail
to see it – Detroit Central becoming
grassland and small farms, embracing
the death of one idea for another.

Or at least I try to believe –
when I am not busy swimming
through tepid lakes of facts. Maybe
nothing will become of the pine cone,
but I can respect that, each cycle,
it is there to be tried.

Flaming Hula Hoops for Peace

I am washing dishes when your brother-in-law tells us
his niece is travelling the world, twirling
flaming hula hoops for peace. Wake up 2 U,
she calls it, her troubadour's demand
over a pounding soundtrack, her 20-year-old face
a wobbly glow of bliss.
We watch it online.

I think of *The Seventh Seal*, the knight's attendant
traipsing wisdom about death's door.

Her uncle worries that it's on the Internet,
an indelible echo.

I wash dishes all afternoon,
each course of a family dinner
demanding more soap and water.
Cleanliness is essential
in such a small house. We are bound
to run out of cups.

In my last school play, I forgot the lines to
Beauty School Dropout, my white spectre,
silver buckled, shuffling up a cirrus of stairs
into a mumbled heaven and a VHS tape
cast mates made me watch just the once.

Neither radical nor raucous, I remember
over-confidence for just a second,
and the falling back to self, flightless:
no hold but my feet leading me out
of character, out of myth.

A myth needs to be outsized to last.

I have set nothing of value on fire.
I *have* washed a lot of dishes.

Report (Hancock Tower, Chicago)

I follow the lights from the 94th floor
out to the periphery of sight and understand
why Elizabeth Bishop called America *sheer*.
Even in the Mies-black, every steeled edge is sharp,
tower windows more vibrantly luminescent,
the bulk of them essential in the fatherly dark.

Streetlamps unfold the map of Midwestern sky,
miles of nothing to hide – no false alleys,
no chimera of mountain. A declaration.

And I walk that map –
among the conference delegates, the specialists,
the tradeshow booth babes.
The whitened teeth
of every room.

I have brought my microphone, my camera,
and simply listen for four days.
This is always the way, I remember now –
observing not words, but the machines they conceive,
a rattle of tones, then a rhythm refined.

No great *I am* in this acquisition,
just a track of voices that file
away and then back to me again.
And in a clearing among them, the story.

Local Politics

The dictator says he will die a martyr
rather than leave his country.

A neighbour's child negotiates his drum kit
through our clapboard walls.

Our friend Andrew's new-found isolation excites him,
the code of the written word cracking in his hands.

I tuck my lover into bed at 10:30,
jimmy the latch of a new novel.

Nights are sometimes a debate
between youth and community. Here comes the solo.

The dictator says over and over
how much his people love him.

Andrew says, what if the royal family were monkeys?
Dressing them to our taste, they'd make a perfect circus.

We could send a letter of complaint, but to what end?
The cat closes his eyes to the tap-tapping, yawns, sneezes.

Following his lead, we wrap him in a blanket,
cut his nails, tidy the sharp edges.

The Cultured Pearl

Of course we are shaped
by the rough tongue of the world.
In a year, even a month,
you can work at your wheel,
your pedals, your desk,
until, for certain, you're through.

Then, uncurl a hand to reveal
what you think is your heart.
It might only be a thumbprint,
a toenail clipping. Do not unravel,
it is only one of many surprises,
a sad, pretty little stone.

But where is the strand,
and how will you hang it
around your neck?

Practicing

A famous musician once explained
death to his daughter by saying
it's like taking off your coat,
and he had her practice with him
shedding the superfluous fabric, striding
across the room of the new self,

as I have done each day this winter –
removing first my hat, surrendering
that symbol of both piety and disguise,
then my scarf's coddling threads.
Next, each tapered finger of glove,
to better feel the way out or into this place.

The coat might be the last barrier
reining in the spirit from wanderlust,
though I slip off with reverence
my chastened boots as well –
the feet, after all, will likely be first
to claim the other side.

While this rite calms me each p.m., I worry
I'll end up cracking a kneecap at the gate
or turnstile, or the same bureau I picture
my failing old body collapsing against.
And as the breath leaves the dusty corpse,
my naked new self will be left to curse the air,
words less satisfying than they once were,
stripped of their echo, their spit.

Afternoon at the Museum

after El Anatsui's Straying Continents

I.
The tin tapestry tangles
a glint across a gallery-sized wall,
copper-clasped bottle caps
cascading to create continents
rending apart along the thin limbs
of a green glass's twist-off tie.
Klimt comes to mind – gold
and shined depth piling on
a breadth of telling light.

II.
Across the street is a dermatologist I visited twice
to have my face soldered clean of veins.
The laser burned, ablating all the red lines
of red wine, misapplied lotion, snow blindness.

The doctor in his pallid mask of eyes and mouth
joked about men and their tears. No smile.
I would return, thinking myself a starter canvas,
ragdoll white. I thought of half-year visits,
special ointments, exotic cleanses, and then
the dentist, the physical, the physio, the flossing,
applying the suntan oil at least twice a day.

Why is preservation always a taking away, and
where did we ever get the idea of completion?
I think of never throwing out anything again.
I dream of cutting my nails and hair, claiming them
in condensed soup cans and cola bottles.

III.

You want to wend your way through
the rest of the gallery, impatient with me
meandering back and forth from these continents
to the plastic pylon of description at its base.

The mass of it could wrap around us
twice or thrice if we could unhasp it from the wall,
but I can only grasp it inside, a river of colour
sintering a map on the underside of my skin.

I think, maybe it will make me beautiful.
That is all I want.

Common Law

Peculiar bridesmaid, conference attendee
suited and muted, past ten on a Tuesday night,
holding a clutch of gerbera, rose and lily,
short a procession in the parking lot's light.

The caterer requested we deflower
the room, sneering, *Haven't you got wives?*
A stalk in my fist, palmed orange and copper
I realized I have, with surprise.

I grab a tissue box to file the spray
of gerber-eyed sneeze in the car's front seat.
To think, it took a second-hand bouquet
to corroborate a fait accompli.

I'd never have gotten here with forethought.
You commend me for what I couldn't have bought.

Suburban Inlet: A Nocturne for Two Voices

The flipper lands loudly, top side of the sheets,
a small seal grunting, snuffling her dream.
A Galapagos or Australian, nudging the breeze?
molting as she bathes in night's cool steam.

Among our bay of houses
behind a reef of lawns
cat and man-boy gambol, scheming
as our lover falls asleep.

I'm reading the fate of the pugnacious sperm whale
in the thick blades and broad chests of Nantucket ships,
riding a black sea of Victorian words,
cautious of her wriggling in our bed's seaward pitch.

Does she hear the sonar pulse of us
stacking plates, the static, the fur against
gadabout leg? We are both sub-mariners now,
I say, the unholy packed away
in our watery skins.

But she's a fine pinniped of the tickling kind
and clocks me not adrift on my whaler's mast,
calls for a delicate scratch of nail
on sleek upper fin and patient back.

A bed of tamed anemones bruises her
to sleep most nights, while man-cat and boy
lick the kitchen clean of sand,
watching for the coelacanth
and our other sightless brothers.

Sleek upper fin and patient back
has been a weakness of mine in all kinds of weather.
Holding her in this fair wind's tack,
I think, maybe this time I'll keep it together.

We listen as young dolphins
leave the bars, the flood
of their tails rousing the street.
Youth in its thimble jar, *I say,*
and the cat turns away.

Circle me, circle me she calls from the beach,
so my hand lazily pendulums her starboard side.
But with a shrug she dives and with her breach, says,
Imagine it a feather plucked to tame sleep's bride.

Boy-cat and kitten claw-tip to bed
whiskering her face an iridescent peck.
A chorused purr, thick as any ocean, rolls
beachward. The guards sleep,
their tridents acquiesce.

Concentration, she opines, *is clearly what you lack,*
so I double my resolve in the muddy green light,
my arm a stylus morsing the sea's unvinyled calls,
the whale's coo and bellow made delicate, slight.

Here is your small barque of animals,
our shining coats, trim paws,
the pads of our feet kneading
the salt-rich dark.

The art of pleasure is reduction
she burbles in my ear,
as my finger traces tightly
the space where she disappears.

Endnotes

Little Empire: John "Jack" Chambers (1931-1978) was a Canadian artist and filmmaker. Born in London, Ontario, Chambers' painting style shifted from surrealist-influenced to photo-realist. In 1969 he was diagnosed with leukemia. *Lunch* is considered his unfinished masterpiece.

The Artist's Son Speaks of Love: This poem was inspired by an interview with one of Alice Neel's sons in the documentary *Neel* (SeeThink Productions). None of it is a direct quotation, however.

Memory: This poem references Mary Oliver's poem "Bone" from the book *Why I Wake Early* (Beacon Press, 2004).

The Emperor, Now a Citizen, Digs His First Hole: This poem was inspired by Bernardo Bertolucci's film, *The Last Emperor* (1987).

Caught: Sir Stanley Spencer (1891-1959) was an English painter. Much of his work depicts Biblical scenes happening not in the Holy Land but in the small Thames-side village of Cookham, where he was born and spent most of his life. This poem is strictly metaphorical. My friend Andrew is a perfectly likeable shut-in and translator who prefers that the authors he translates be at least 50 years dead.

Packing for a conference: August Kleinzahler, Mary Oliver and Ted Kooser are all contemporary American poets.

Dr. Tsien Responds to His Biographers: Dr. Tsien Hsue-shen was an important figure in the history of the birth of the space age, having laid the foundation for the Jet Propulsion Laboratory in Pasadena, CA. In 1955, he was deported from the United States and returned to his birthplace, China, where he was important in the development of the country's missile program. The poem was inspired by Iris Chang's sensitive and probing biography *Thread of the Silkworm* (Basic Books, 1995).

Herdwick Sheep: The Herdwick is a breed of domestic sheep native to the Lake District of Cumbria in northwest England. The name "Herdwick" is derived from the Old Norse *herdvyck*, meaning sheep pasture. Fell: a local term for mountain. Tups: Herdwick rams. Heaf (also heft): a small local area in which a sheep spends its life; remaining in this area is something a ewe learns from its mother. "Hesket brew" refers to Cumbria's Hesket Newmarket Brewery and its fine wares.

Afternoon at the Museum: El Anatsui's *Straying Continents* was specially commissioned for the Royal Ontario Museum and can be viewed there in all its glory.

Suburban Inlet: The pinniped is an aquatic carnivorous mammal with a body specialized for swimming, and limbs modified as flippers – i.e. seals, walruses and sea lions. I don't recommend comparing your lover to one.

Acknowledgements

My thanks to Allan Briesmaster, for his insightful fine-tuning of this collection; to Meaghan Strimas, for seeing promise in and helping to greatly improve upon earlier drafts of the manuscript; to everyone in the Muse Co-op and Vaughan Poets Circle, for their unfailingly supportive criticism; to Catherine Owen, for introducing me to new voices and offering helpful pointers on sections of this collection; to friends and family, near and far, who continue to support this habit of mine; and to Kristi Edamura Cross, who made the creation of this possible.